A PRACTICAL

HANDBOOK

FOR THE ACTOR

Melissa Bruder   Nathaniel Pollack
Lee Michael Cohn   Robert Previto
Madeleine Olnek   Scott Zigler

With an Introduction by David Mamet

Vintage Books
A Division of Random House   New York

A Vintage Original, May 1986

First Edition

Library of Congress Cataloging-in-Publication Data

A Practical handbook for the actor.

   "A Vintage original"—T.p. verso.
   1. Stanislavsky method. 2. Acting. I. Bruder,
Melissa.
PN2062.P73 1986   792'.028   85-40875
ISBN 0-394-74412-8

Designed by Frederica Templeton
Manufactured in the United States of America

987

Cover photo by Gary Heery

This book is dedicated to W. H. Macy and David Mamet.

"Always tell the truth. It's the easiest thing to remember."

Contents

Introduction

Most acting training is based on shame and guilt. If you have studied acting, you have been asked to do exercises you didn't understand, and when you did them, as your teacher adjudged, badly, you submitted guiltily to the criticism. You have also been asked to do exercises you *did* understand, but whose application to the craft of acting escaped you, and you were ashamed to ask that their usefulness be explained.

As you did these exercises it seemed that everyone around you understood their purpose but you—so, guiltily, you learned to pretend. You learned to pretend to "smell the coffee" when doing sensory exercises. You learned to pretend that the "mirror exercise" was demanding, and that doing it well would somehow make you more attuned on stage. You learned to pretend to "hear the music with your toes," and to "use the space."

As you went from one class to the next and from one teacher to the next, two things happened: being human, your need to believe asserted itself. You were loath to believe your teachers were frauds, so you began to believe that you *yourself* were a fraud. This contempt for yourself became contempt for all those who did not share the particular bent of your school of training.

While keeping up an outward show of perpetual study, you began to believe that no actual, practicable technique of acting existed, and this was the only possible belief supported by the evidence.

Now how do I know these things about you? I know them because I suffered them myself. I suffered them as a longtime student of acting, and as an actor. I suffer them second hand as a teacher of acting, as a director, and as a playwright.

I know that you are dedicated and eager—eager to learn, eager to *believe,* eager to find a way to bring that art that you feel in yourself to the stage. You are legitimately willing to sacrifice, and you think that the sacrifice required of you is subjugation to the will of a teacher. But a more exacting sacrifice is required: you must follow the dictates of your common sense.

It would be fine if there were many great master teachers of acting, but there are not. Most acting teachers, unfortunately, are frauds, and they rely on your complicity to survive. This not only deprives you of positive training but stifles your greatest gift as an artist: your sense of truth. It is this sense of truth, a simplicity, and feelings of wonder and reverence—all of which you possess—that will revitalize the Theatre. How do you translate them onto the Stage?

This book offers some wonderful, simple advice and suggestions. It is the best book on acting written in the last twenty years. The technical suggestions, finally, are reducible to a simple stoic philosophy: be what you wish to seem.

Stanislavsky once wrote that you should "play well or badly, but play truly." It is not up to you whether your performance will be brilliant—all that is under your control is your intention. It is not under your control whether your career will be brilliant—all that is under your control is your intention.

If you intend to manipulate, to show, to impress, you may experience mild suffering and pleasant triumphs. If you intend to follow the truth you feel in yourself— to follow your common sense, and force your will to serve you in the quest for discipline and simplicity— you will subject yourself to profound despair, loneliness, and constant self-doubt. And if you persevere, the Theatre, which you are learning to serve, will grace you, now and then, with the greatest exhilaration it is possible to know.

—David Mamet
Cabot, Vermont
1985

Authors' Note

This book originally evolved from an exercise assigned to us by David Mamet during his summer acting workshop in Montpelier, Vermont, in 1984. The major portion of the text was gleaned from notes taken in David's and W. H. Macy's acting classes during summer workshops in 1983 and 1984 and during the New York University fall and winter sessions in New York and at the Goodman Theatre in Chicago. The Practical Aesthetics Workshop, as the group is officially known, came together under the auspices of New York University and was organized purely as a one-shot summer program. That the workshop has continued for over two years is a testament to the dedication of the teachers and students alike. The final fruit of our study has been the formation of the Atlantic Theatre Company, a company whose members are almost all Practical Aesthetics Workshop alumni.

The authors would like to thank the following individuals for their support and encouragement: Lindsay Crouse, Derek Johns, Bill Macy, David Mamet,

Evangeline Morphos, Gregory Mosher, Robin Speilberg and Linda Miller (typists extraordinaire), Andrew Wylie, and all the members, past and present, of the Atlantic Theatre Company.

Melissa Bruder
Lee Michael Cohn
Madeleine Olnek
Nathaniel Pollack
Robert Previto
Scott Zigler

Vermont
1985

A PRACTICAL
HANDBOOK
FOR THE ACTOR

The Job of the Actor

J. D. Salinger once said, "You were a reader before you were a writer." By the same token, all actors started out as audience members. What were the first things that struck us about the theatre? What are the things that draw us to the theatre again and again? What creates those moments that every audience member has had of sitting up in his chair because something has struck him in the gut? These moments are under no one person's control; their creation is shared in equally by audience, actor, director, and technician. Realizing this, the actor must understand that it is not rational to say, "It is my job to create these magical moments." Instead, he should realize that all he can do is bring himself to the theatre in optimum condition to participate in the play at hand. Identifying what things he can do to put himself in optimum condition and then doing them consistently so that they become habitual to him will give the actor the satisfaction of always knowing what to do, what his job truly is.

The actor will find, however, that while his job may

be clearly identifiable, it will not be easy. For example, to be in optimum condition to do a play, the actor must have a strong, clear, resonant voice. But developing this type of voice takes most people many years of training, of applying the will to working daily on effective vocal exercises. The actor knows he must develop a body that will do whatever is asked of it, but this again requires the discipline to exercise as well as the study of movement so that the body will become as strong, supple, and graceful as the physical constraints within which he was born (about which he can do nothing) will allow. The actor must look at himself honestly, which requires a great deal of bravery, and use his common sense to determine what his own shortcomings are. Then he must determine which of these shortcomings it is within his control to change. Given this, he must devote himself to doing everything he can to correct those things within his control; he must use his will to become to the fullest possible extent that person he would ideally like to be. Then when he comes to the theatre, he can have the satisfaction of saying to himself, "I know exactly what my job is. I have done everything in my power to be ready to go onstage." This will free him to be more completely involved with the play as it unfolds onstage, because he will not be worrying about what he could have done to be more prepared.

The best thing you can do for yourself as an actor is to clearly define and list those things that *are* your responsibilities and separate them from those things that are *not*. In other words, itemize what is within your control and what is not. If you apply this rather stoic philosophy of working on only those things within your control and not concerning yourself with those things that are not, then every moment you spend will be concretely contributing to your growth as an actor. Why not devote your time and energy to developing measurable skills such as your voice, your ability to analyze a script correctly, your ability to concentrate, and your body? On the other hand, how can it possibly help to concern yourself with the views others choose to take of you, the overall success or failure of the play, the ability (or lack thereof) of the director or other actors, which critics are sitting in the audience, your height, your feelings, and so forth? You cannot and never will be able to do anything about any of these things. Consequently, it makes sense to devote yourself only to those things which you have the capacity to change, and refrain from wasting your time, thought, and energy on these things you can never affect.

As an actor, you should never concern yourself with "talent." Talent, if it exists at all, is completely out of your control. Whatever talent might be, you either have it or you don't, so why waste energy worrying about it? The only talent you need to act is a talent for working—in other words, the ability to apply yourself in learning the skills that make up the craft of acting. To put it simply, anyone can act if he has the will to do so, and anyone who says he wants to but doesn't have the knack for it suffers from a lack of will, not a lack of talent.

Another major part of the actor's job is to find a way to live truthfully under the imaginary circumstances of the play. Thus the actor must be able to decide what is going on in the text in simple, actable terms. If the actor gives himself something physically doable that he has a personal investment in for every scene, he will always have something more important to put his attention on than the success or failure of his own performance. Again, the actor must use his common sense to identify what is and is not within his control. Your feelings are not within your control, so it is not within the bounds of common sense to say "I must feel this certain way" for any particular moment of the scene. Instead, you must be able to say, "This is what I am *doing* in the scene, and I will do it irrespective of how it makes me feel."

You must understand that acting, like carpentry, is a craft with a definite set of skills and tools. By assiduously applying your will to the acquiring of those skills and tools, you will eventually make them habitual. Once your skills become habitual, you need no longer concentrate on your technique; the craft you have developed will work *for* you and allow you to operate freely within its bounds. For example, if you have worked long and hard on your voice, then you are free to put your attention on what is going on in the scene rather than on being heard.

If this sounds like an awful lot, it is. Acting requires common sense, bravery, and a lot of will: the *common sense* to translate whatever you are given into simple actable terms; the *bravery* to throw yourself into the action of the play despite fear of failure, self-consciousness, and a thousand other obstacles; and the *will* to adhere to your ideals, even though it might not be the easiest thing to do.

In our world it is becoming harder and harder to

communicate with each other simply and honestly, on a gut level. Yet we still go to the theatre to have a communion with the truth of our existence, and, ideally, we leave it knowing that that kind of communication is still possible. The theatre can put forward simple human values in hopes that the audience may leave inspired to try to live by such values. Seeing an individual doing his best against impossible odds and without regard to his fears allows the audience to identify that very capacity within themselves. That iron will is the will of the actor bringing not some "magnificent performance" to the stage, but his own simple human values and the actions to which they drive him. When truth and virtue are so rare in almost every area of our society the world *needs* theatre and the theatre needs actors who will bring the truth of the human soul to the stage. The theatre may now be the only place in society where people can go to hear the truth.

Technique Outline

Technique is a knowledge of the tools that may be used for a certain craft and an understanding of how to apply those tools. In carpentry, the carpenter first learns what the tools of his craft are and then how to use those tools to build things. Similarly, the actor must learn what the tools at his disposal are and then how he can utilize these tools in doing a play. This knowledge is his technique.

Acting is living truthfully under the imaginary circumstances of a play. It can be broken down into two areas: *action* and *moment*. Action is what you go onstage to do, the physical process of trying to obtain a specific goal, often referred to as the objective. Moment is what is actually happening in the scene as you are playing it at any given instant. Ideally, every moment of a play is based on what has happened in the moment preceding it. Acting then is dealing truthfully with the other actors onstage in order to pursue a specific goal. The actor should *prepare* so that he can *improvise* onstage while sticking to certain given circumstances.

Given circumstances are anything set forth by the writer or director that must be adhered to by the actor. The location of the action of the play and everything that this suggests—for example, dialects, costumes, or scenery—is a given circumstance. Any physicality specified for a character by the playwright—a limp or a hunchback, for example—is also a given circumstance. Finally, anything asked for by the director, from specific blocking to crying or yelling at a certain moment, is a given circumstance and must be respected by the actor as such. In some instances the director may choose to supplant some of the given circumstances of the play, such as the location or time period, with his own ideas. In these cases the actor should simply accept the director's changes as the given circumstances of the play. Acting can then be looked at as improvising within this framework of given circumstances.

The preparation is the work the actor does with the script to find the action of a given scene (see chapters 1 and 2, "Physical Action" and "Analyzing a Scene"). The improvisation is the act of impulsively choosing from moment to moment how to do that action, and these choices are based on what is going on in the other actors in the scene at that instant (see chapter 3, "The Truth of the Moment"). This may sound simple, but there is nothing easy about finding a strong, playable action for a scene, nor is it easy to see what is going on in another person and to act on those observations impulsively. These are skills that can only be developed by years of practice. The actor must understand that a technique cannot in itself enable him or her to act. Rather, it provides the actor with tools that, combined with strength of will, bravery, and common sense, can help the actor bring the life of the human soul to the circumstances created by the playwright.

The first part of this book is a presentation and explanation of the tools the actor has at his disposal. The more habitual the use of these tools becomes, the easier it will be for the actor to deal with the pitfalls of the professional theatre discussed in the second half of this book. The training process is nothing more than the process of making the use of these tools habitual, just as the rehearsal process is primarily for habituating the actor to the actions he has chosen for the play. Once these things are habitual, the actor need not think about them. Only then is he free to play.

Part One

THE TECHNIQUE

THE TECHNIQUE

1

Physical Action

To act means to do, so you must always have something specific to *do* onstage or you will immediately stop acting. This is why physical action is so very important for the actor. Simply defined, an *action* is the physical pursuance of a specific goal. Physical action is the main building block of an actor's technique because it is the one thing that you, the actor, can consistently *do* onstage. Choosing a good action is an invaluable skill that can only be developed by long, hard practice. In this chapter you will find the requirements of a good action; use them as a checklist when figuring out an action for any scene.

An action must

1. be physically capable of being done.
2. be fun to do.
3. be specific.
4. have its test in the other person.
5. not be an errand.
6. not presuppose any physical or emotional state.

7. not be manipulative.
8. have a "cap."
9. be in line with the intentions of the playwright.

1. An action must be *physically capable of being done.* At any moment you should be able to begin doing it. For example, "pleading for help" is something you can begin to do immediately. Everyone knows how to do it. On the other hand, "pursuing the American dream" is not something you can pick up and *do* at a moment's notice. To say something is physically capable of being done does not necessarily involve intense physical activity such as jumping up and down or assaulting someone. Pleading for help can be accomplished while sitting absolutely still in a chair. *An action must be something that you, the actor, can actually accomplish onstage.*

2. An action must be *fun to do.* As you will discover in scene analysis (see chapter 2), any number of actions can be correct for a particular scene. Common sense dictates that you figure out the one you as an actor will *want* to do, since you are the one who will have to do it every night of the week. By fun we don't necessarily mean something that makes you laugh, but something that is truly compelling to you. This includes things you might never actually do offstage, but that appeal to your *sense of play.* If you've ever really wanted to tell someone off, for instance, here is your chance. Language is your main tool here. The more vital, active, and gutsy your language is, the more life you will bring to the stage because your action will be that much more exciting to you. How much more fun it is to "talk a friend into spilling the beans" than to "get someone to give me information." There will occasionally be times when a seemingly mundane action is perfectly correct for a scene. The point is to find the action you *want* to do. What gets you going? What gets you hot? Only you know. The way you speak to yourself is the way you will act. If you are clear, specific, and strong with yourself, then, chances are that that is how you will be onstage.

3. An action must be *specific*. Stanislavsky said, "Generality is the enemy of all art," and nothing could be truer. If your action is in general, then everything you do onstage will be in general. The specificity of an action such as "extracting a crucial answer" will bring you to life much more than the vagueness of "finding out something." Furthermore, a specific action will provide you with a clear, specific path to follow when playing the scene.

4. *The test of the action must be in the other person.* An action is the physical pursuance of a specific goal, and that specific goal must have to do with the other person. In other words, by looking at your partner, you should be able to tell how close you are to completing your action. This will also make you less self-conscious and allow you to concentrate on something infinitely more interesting than how well you are performing—that person across from you. If your action is "forcing an enemy to do my bidding," at any moment you should be able to tell how close he is to doing your bidding, and

only when he has done your bidding will you have completed the action.

5. An action *cannot be an errand.* An errand is an action that has no test in the other person. "Delivering a message" is not a good action because you do not have to look at your partner to see if you have accomplished it. Also, it can be accomplished in one line, leaving you with nothing to do for the rest of the scene. If you pick an action that keeps you working off the other person to achieve it, you will be brought to life throughout the scene. Too quickly and easily accomplished, an errand is boring both for you to perform and for the audience to watch. The action must be something it is possible to fail at; you cannot fail at an errand.

6. An action *cannot presuppose any physical or emotional state,* either in you or in your partner. You can't artificially induce a physical or emotional state (e.g., hunger, anger, sorrow, drunkenness), because they are not within your control. Any action requiring you to put yourself into a certain state before or during a scene will force you to act a lie, the truth being that you are not actually in that state. If you try to work yourself up into a certain state for a scene, your attention will be entirely on the creation and maintenance of that state rather than on your action. As will be discussed later in detail, there is no such thing as a correct emotion for any scene. "Making a jerk know how mad I am" is a bad action because you cannot do it unless you are angry. A better action would be "putting a jerk in his place."

The same holds true for your partner. "Calming

down an excited friend" will not work because if the person in front of you is not excited, then you have nothing to play. "Building up a friend's confidence" is a better choice because it does not presuppose your friend's physical or emotional state; you can always build someone's confidence higher than it already is.

7. An action *cannot be manipulative.* A manipulative action is one chosen to produce a desired effect on your partner. This type of action gives rise to the attitude that "I can do whatever I want to you, but nothing you do is going to affect me." In other words, you make up your mind ahead of time how you are going to play the scene and allow nothing to sway you. An action such as "making someone cry" is manipulative. An action such as "forcing a friend to face facts" might very well make your partner cry, but the crying is more likely to be the honest response to your carrying out your action, rather than the result of your manipulation. A manipulative action can cause you to act in a predetermined way instead of dealing truthfully with what is happening in the other person (see chapter 3 on "The Truth of the Moment").

8. The action *must have a "cap."* The cap is that specific thing you are looking for that will mean that you have succeeded at your action. You must be able to tell whether or not you have finished doing your action by looking at the other person. For example, "to get a friend's forgiveness" is an action with a cap. You *know* when your partner has forgiven you by his behavior toward you. On the other hand, an action such as "maintaining someone's interest" does not have a cap. Depending on the scene, you may never actually achieve your action, but you must always have a specific *end* to work toward onstage.

9. The action must be *in line with the intentions of the playwright*. This is extremely important, and can be better understood in conjunction with scene analysis. Once you have determined exactly what the playwright's intentions are, the actions you choose must be true to those intentions. For example, in Arthur Miller's *Death of a Salesman*, in the scene where Willy returns home after his harrowing trip, if the actress playing Linda chooses an action such as "putting someone in his place" for the scene, it is clearly out of whack with the intentions of the playwright. Something more in line with the scene would be "assuring a loved one of my support."

Within each action is an infinite number of *tools*, or ways to go about executing that action. For instance, if your action is "to get a straight answer," at various points in the scene you might demand, cajole, reason with, intimidate, or threaten the other person to get the answer. After you have analyzed a scene try listing some of the tools you can use to go about getting what you want. The right tool is, as you will learn later on, mainly dictated by what the other person in the scene is doing.

2

Analyzing a Scene

Now that you know what a good action entails, you must learn to choose the best action for a scene. The following simple formula, if employed consistently, will always lead to a performable action in line with the intentions of the playwright. Ask yourself these three questions:

1. What is the character literally doing?

2. What is the essential action of what the character is doing in this scene?

3. What is that action like to me? *It's as if* . . .

1. What is the character literally doing? The key to answering this question is to be as literal as possible; do not interpret or embellish what is happening on the printed page. A character may say and do many things in a scene, some of them seemingly contradictory. Your task is to find out the one specific thing he is doing that encompasses *every line*. Phrase what the character is doing in a single, precise sentence, and do not omit any lines, no matter how incongruous a particular line or section might seem.

Here is an example: A man enters a room, reaches for his pipe, searches for his tobacco pouch, takes his tobacco pouch from his desk drawer, opens the pouch, fills the pipe, and takes out his matches. What the character is literally doing is *preparing to smoke his pipe*. Even if we add that the character settles into his easy chair and puts a record on the turntable, what the character is doing remains the same; settling into a favorite chair and playing his favorite music are still part of preparing to smoke his pipe.

As mundane as this may seem, correctly analyzing what the character is doing is vital to finding a good action in a scene. Also, correctly defining what the character is doing will help to keep you in accord with the playwright's intentions throughout the rest of the analysis. What the character is doing does not have to be exciting to you as an actor because this will never be your action onstage. Rather, your answer to question 1 of the analysis must be accurate, so don't worry about following any of the guidelines in chapter 1. You must remember that for the purpose of analysis the character exists only on the printed page. Thus the answers to this question should always be put in the third person.

2. What is the essential action of what the character is doing in this scene? Once you know what the character is literally doing, the next step is choosing the essential action, or essence, of what the character is doing in the scene. This is the actual physical action you will be performing onstage as outlined in chapter 2. The action is the *essential* aspect of what the character is doing. For example, in act 2, scene 3 of *Golden Boy* by Clifford Odets:

What is the character literally doing?
1. Joe is getting Lorna to dump Moody and become his girl.
2. The essential action of that is: *Making a loved one take a big chance.*

By getting to the essential action of what the character is doing, the actor has stripped away the emotional connotations that might be suggested by the given circumstances of the play. For example, in this scene Joe is in love with Lorna, but the essential action is getting her to take the chance. By concentrating on getting her to do something, and not on trying to be in love for the duration of the scene, the actor will find himself in the world of the concretely doable, not in the nebulous world of feelings outside the actor's control. The essential action, then, is what exists in the scene when you eliminate all ideas about what you think the author is saying the character feels at any given moment in favor of what he is trying to accomplish. The idea of Lorna dumping Moody for Joe involves all the emotional aspects of a romantic triangle, but what is essential as an end result is one person trying to get another person to take a chance.

The scene definitely will have an emotional life, but one spontaneously born out of the actor's experience of trying to accomplish something, the degree to which he succeeds or fails, and his reactions to the other person while he is trying to fulfill his action. The actor does not need to think about or work for these things. If he really throws himself into getting the other person to take a chance, the audience will believe he is driven by his love because of the given circumstances of the play, even though the reasons he gives himself for doing it may have nothing to do with love, as will be explained in the next section of this chapter. The actor doesn't need to remind the audience of what the circumstances are, so all that is left for him to do is to illustrate that part of the scene not taken care of by the lines—the physical act of carrying out the essential action of the scene.

The essential action must conform to the guidelines set forth in the previous chapter. Whereas in Step 1 you said to yourself, "What is the character literally doing?" in this step you ask yourself, "What am *I* going to do onstage?"

Let's look at the character of Happy in *Death of a Salesman*. In act 1, scene 2, Happy is upstairs talking with his brother Biff, having been waked up by his father rustling about downstairs. In the scene Happy

- breaks the ice with Biff after a long separation.
- gets Biff to open up.
- fills Biff in on what's been going on since he has been away.
- tries to find out what Biff is doing with his life.
- expresses his dissatisfaction with his own life.
- considers Biff's business proposal.

When we tie these components together, what the character is doing is *having a heart-to-heart talk with his brother*. The essence of what the character is doing in the scene might be, for example, *putting a loved one on the right track*. The tools* you might use to execute this action are: hear out, scold, level with, teach a lesson, and so forth.

No one essential action is engraved in stone for each scene. You must decide for yourself the best action for a particular scene, keeping in mind the guidelines in chapter 1. That we are now applying the concept of physical action to a scene in a play does not alter the fact that the action must be physically capable of being done, fun to do, testable in the other person, etc. As you will see, the employment of a good action within the strictures of a script brings the actor, and thus the play, to life.

You can perform only one action at a time, so the one you choose must be appropriate for the *entire* scene. If you can't distill it down to one action, either you need to do some more analysis or the scene needs to be broken down into several different actions, or beats. A beat is a single unit of action, and a beat change is the point where a new action begins. A beat change occurs when a new piece of information is introduced or an event takes place over which the character has no control and which by its very nature must change what he is doing. This is not to be confused with trying to exe-

---

*The word "tool" is used quite often in this book. For the sake of clarity, we wish to point out that this word is used in two ways: the basic tools that comprise the craft of acting, such as voice, the ability to analyze a scene, and so forth; and the tools of a specific action.

cute the same action in a different way, i.e., employing a different tool. (An example of a beat change is discussed in scene 2 of the analysis model of *Oedipus Rex*.)

Here are a few examples of some actions and how they serve a given scene. Here is Stanley Kowalski's famous "Stella!" scene (act 5, scene 3) from Tennessee Williams' *Streetcar Named Desire*:

. . . .

STANLEY: Stella! (There is a pause) My baby doll's left me! (He breaks into sobs. Then he goes to the phone and dials, still shuddering with sobs.) Eunice? I want my baby. (He waits a moment; then he hangs up and dials again.) Eunice! I'll keep on ringin' until I talk with my baby! (. . . He hurls the phone to the floor . . . Finally Stanley stumbles half dressed out to the porch and down the wooden steps to the pavement before the building. There he throws back his head like a baying hound and bellows his wife's name: "Stella! Stella! Sweetheart! Stella!") Stanley: Stell-lahhhh!

EUNICE: (calling down from the door of her upper apartment): Quit that howling out there an' go back to bed!

STANLEY: I want my baby down here. Stella, Stella!

EUNICE: She ain't comin' down, so you quit! Or you'll git th' law on you!

STANLEY: Stella!

EUNICE: You can't beat on a woman an' then call 'er back! She won't come! And her goin' t' have a baby! . . . You stinker! You whelp of a Polack, you! I hope they do haul you in and turn the firehouse on you, same as last time!

STANLEY (humbly): Eunice, I want my girl to come down with me!

EUNICE: Hah! (She slams her door.)
STANLEY (with heaven-splitting violence): STELL-
    LAHHHHH! (. . . The door upstairs opens again.
    Stella slips down the rickety stairs in her robe
    . . . they come together . . .

1. *What is the character literally doing?* We decided
   that Stanley was *screaming for Stella to come
   home to him.* You might have a different way of
   phrasing this; for the sake of this example, let's
   assume that this is the most accurate description
   of Stanley's lines.

2. *What is the essential action of what the character
   is doing in this scene?* Here are only a few of the
   possible actions that could work in this scene:
   a. to beg a loved one's forgiveness.
   b. to clear up a terrible misunderstanding.
   c. to retrieve what is rightfully mine.
   d. to implore a loved one to give me another
      chance.
   e. to show an inferior who's boss.
   f. to make amends for bad behavior.

All of the above actions, despite their variation, could
each serve the needs of the scene. Notice that each one
is phrased clearly and concisely, thus making it easy to
act on. Further, each one conforms to the guidelines in
chapter 1. As per examples c and d, an action is always
phrased in the first person. Finally, in the action where
another person is mentioned, the relationship will to a
great degree dictate how the action will be performed.
   Be extremely specific when including the nature of

the relationship in your action. In the case of Stanley
and Stella, the *characters* are husband and wife. However, in a given situation, husband and wife can be pals,
adversaries, best friends, lovers, student and teacher, or
rivals, just to name a few. Just as you choose the essence
of the action specifically, you must define for yourself
the nature of the relationship with equal specificity because it will make the action that much more meaning-
ful to you. Again, the question to ask yourself is, What
do husband and wife mean in this particular scene?
Because you will know *who* you are dealing with in the
scene, you will have a much clearer idea how to go
about executing your action. Remember that the nature of a single relationship in a play may change from
scene to scene. In *Streetcar,* Stanley and Stella may be
lovers in one scene and sworn enemies in another.

Sometimes the nature of the relationship is clearly
defined by the playwright. In these cases, you need not
include the nature of the relationship in your analysis
because it will not affect the way you will execute the
action. You must use your judgment each time you
analyze a scene concerning whether to include the nature of the relationship.

The action must not be a simple restating of the answer to the first question, What is the character literally
doing? This is because you will never be able to *believe*
that you are the character that you are playing. It is
simply not possible, unless you are dangerously
psychotic, and if that is the case, this book will be of
little use to you. If you are called upon to actually believe that you are Stanley Kowalski and the actress playing Stella is your wife, sooner or later your intellect will

rebel at the suggestion; you cannot play tricks on your rational mind. The purpose of physical action is to give you something more interesting, important, and fun to concentrate on than trying to believe the fiction of the script. As you will see in chapter 10, you will never have to worry about creating the character you are playing because most of that is taken care of for you in the script.

For instance, if Stanley is, as we previously decided, *screaming for Stella to come home to him* and you choose *demanding that a loved one return*, you have simply reiterated the answer to question 1 using slightly different words. Thus you have not made a specific choice and will have to depend on the lines to get you through the scene. The difference between the action you choose and the character's action creates a dynamic between the lines of the script and what you are doing on stage. This dynamic is part of what creates the illusion of character in the eyes of the audience (see chapter 10), what brings the scene to life.

A good action will help you bring your own personality to bear on the role because you will have chosen exactly what you will be doing. Finding and sticking to a good action is extremely important. It is your most powerful tool as an actor.

3. What does this action mean to me? It's as if . . . The third step in the process of scene analysis involves the use of the actor's imagination. As you will see, the "as-if" serves several crucial purposes and is the logical completion of the analysis process. It helps the actor gain a fuller understanding of the action he has chosen for a given scene. It also gives the actor a clear sense of the consequences of not completing his action—that is to say, it sets the stakes in the playing of the scene. This is especially important in terms of staying true to the playwright's intentions. Finally, the as-if reinforces the actor's sense of play, which is vital to his work.

The way to achieve the above-mentioned benefits is not by investing in an emotional state, but by creating for yourself a tangible, personal stake in the action you have chosen. The means of bringing the action home to you is the as-if. It is a simple mnemonic device, a suggestion by means of which you remind yourself of what the action means to you in personal terms. It should be a simple, fun (and again, we do mean compelling) fantasy in which you use your imagination in a way you can readily accept. For example, creating an as-if in which you are infiltrating the Nazi forces that have abducted your family may be an interesting fantasy, but unless you have experience as an international spy, the as-if will not work because you have no idea what to actually physically do in that situation. In other words, it's not something you can act on. Using again the example of Stanley Kowalski, here are a few examples of good as-ifs:

1. *What is the character literally doing?* Screaming for Stella to come home to him. (This step will remain the same for the following actions and as-ifs.)

2. *What is the essential action of what the character is doing in this scene?* To beg a loved one's forgiveness.

3. *What is that action like to me? It's as if* I broke my mother's prized family heirloom and she threw me out of the house. To be allowed back into my house I must *beg her forgiveness.*

This is a good as-if for several reasons. First, it is something that could happen. Thus I can accept it unquestioningly and act upon it immediately. Second, it is simple and direct, and does not complicate the action. Third, it is in line with the intentions of the playwright because the stakes are high: if I don't get my mother's forgiveness something terrible will happen—I will be banned from my home. In the scene, if Stanley doesn't convince Stella to come home to him, he too will incur a terrible loss.

An as-if should be no more than two or three simple sentences in order to keep it readily accessible to you. It should have enough details to spark your imagination, but not so many as to form in effect a substitute for the scene. If the above as-if had been phrased simply "It's as if I had fight with my mother," it would have been ineffective. Two details—breaking the heirloom and being thrown out of the house—make it *personal* and place it in adjustment with the stakes of the scene.

Here are the aforementioned actions and their possible as-ifs:

action: to clear up a terrible misunderstanding.
as if: I were sitting in a hot tub nude with a female friend, and her boyfriend walked in and thought we were fooling around. I then explain to him that nothing was going on behind his back.

action: to retrieve what is rightfully mine.

as if: I am demanding that my stepmother turn over to my sister and me property left to us after our father's death that she is trying to cheat us out of.

action: to implore a loved one to give me another chance.

as if: I'm persuading my fiancée not to break off our relationship after she discovered I had an affair while she was away.

action: to show an inferior who's boss.

as if: my new secretary started reeling off her rules to me the first day on the job and I told her she'd better follow my rules or she'd be looking for a new job.

action: to make amends for bad behavior.

as if: I'm apologizing to my best friend's parents for showing up roaring drunk at their twenty-fifth anniversary party and making a loud-mouthed ass of myself.

Remember that the as-if is purely a memory device, a way of sparking yourself to invest fully in the scene. *Under no circumstances* should you ever play the as-if onstage. It is not a substitute for the play; it is something you have created for yourself to both personalize the action and get your motor going. That the as-if's are extremely different from the content of the scene is no accident. The as-if is there to get you *away* from the scene, away from the fiction of the script so that you can find parallels directly accessible to you and thus easy to act on. Once you have used the as-if to personally invest in a given scene, the lines and attendant physical activity therein are simply tools to aid you in executing your action.

The great debate throughout the history of acting is whether the actor must feel what his or her character is ostensibly feeling at any given moment. The bottom line is: What does it look like to the audience? The crucial thing to remember is that the actor is not on-stage to have an experience or to expose himself to the audience, but to help tell a story. At a certain point the playwright may require an actress to sob over the death of the lover of the character she is playing. All that is necessary is that the audience believe you are upset. The audience will not know what you have said you are doing in your analysis. You may be playing a scene in which your character is dealing with his girlfriend, but your as-if has to do with your brother. What the audience sees is someone with a need to get something from the other person in the scene, and its understanding of that need will be based on the elements of the play, since that is the only information it has to go on. The audience comes to the theatre set to believe the story. The actor comes to the theatre to help tell the story, not by tricking himself into believing things he knows aren't true, but by applying the tools he has developed to create an illusion.

Now that we have described the elements comprising a good as-if, here are the major pitfalls to guard against when you begin to use your imagination in this very disciplined manner.

Be wary of as-ifs that are too close to your personal life. For certain people something incredibly emotional, such as the recent death of a loved one, is not

good material for an as-if because it will close them off.
If you feel personally violated by exposing your feelings
about such an event, or if it is simply too overwhelming
to deal with in the context of your work, it is not good
as-if material. The as-if is there to help you invest in the
work, not to dredge your intimate secrets out of you.
The actor's job is not to bring the truth of his personal
life to the stage, but rather to bring the truth of himself
to the specific needs of the play. We have found that
as-if's based on a desire to in some way aid *someone else*
are highly effective and a great deal of fun.

In order to create a good as-if you must use your
imagination, not simply reiterate the events of the
scene. For instance, if the scene concerns a character
breaking the news of his father's death to his mother,
do not use an as-if in which you are doing just that. If
you do, your work will become generalized, because by
attempting to render what is on the printed page, you
will have fallen into the trap of playing the character.
Also, as previously mentioned, you don't want to put
your concentration back on the imaginary circumstances because you don't want to put yourself in the
position of having to believe the fiction of the script.

It is wise to avoid some subjects in creating an as-if.
We can't tell you exactly what they are because they
differ from person to person. We do suggest, however,
that you avoid anything that is a drudgery in your daily
life—anything that makes you say "ugh!" or "not that
again!" Choose things that get you hot. Why have a
Class B fantasy when you can have a Class A? Choose
something that makes you really want to act the action
you have chosen for the scene. Take the time to dis-

cover what you really care about, what you would really love to do if you had the chance. In other words, PLAY! The better your as-if, the stronger your action, and thus the full strength of your humanity will be brought to the work.

. . .

The principles involved in analyzing an entire play are the same as those involved in analyzing a single scene. The only additional concept is that of *through-action*, or *through-line*. By this we mean the single overriding action that all the individual actions serve. You must decide what your ultimate goal is and then construct each individual action to bring you a step closer to achieving that goal. Sometimes you might find it difficult to grasp your through-action immediately. If that is the case, simply break the play down into its individual components and then extrapolate from those actions the single idea uniting them. That single idea, once it has been put within the context of the analysis formula, is the through-line of the role you are playing.

However you find your through-action, you must do a complete three-step analysis that is as precise and thorough as that for the individual actions. The through-action will provide a means by which to gauge the strength and accuracy of each individual action. A through-action can be somewhat broader than an action you would play in a scene because you never actually play it onstage. It exists to unify the individual beats you have chosen. For instance, if you are playing the ingenue role in *42nd Street*, a very good through-action might be "to make the dream of a lifetime come true." Also, a hot as-if will set stakes and personalize the role for you. On the other hand, "to make the dream of a lifetime come true" is too broad to use for a single scene because it doesn't conform to several of the guidelines discussed in chapter 1. Remember that the correct unit for an actor's concentration is the scene. Your job is to accomplish one action at a time; if you attempt to act the through-action you will dilute the specificity of your analysis of each scene. The through-action exists as an analysis tool only. The following analysis of *Oedipus Rex* illustrates the concept of through-action and its relationship to the individual beats of the play.

CHARACTER: Oedipus

Prologue
  What the character does:
    Oedipus tells the people of Thebes that he's doing all he can to conquer the plague.
    Oedipus gets information from Creon on what the oracle said to do.
    Oedipus says he'll do all he can.
  Analysis:
    1. Oedipus is doing everything he can think of to deal with the plague.
    2. Reassuring people in my care that I'm capable of getting the job done.
  Tools:
    To pacify, explain, take charge, promise, appease.

Scene 1
  What the character does:
    Oedipus curses the murderer and all who help him.

Oedipus makes Teiresias tell him what he knows.
Oedipus accuses Teiresias of conspiring with Creon.
Oedipus tries to get information.
Oedipus tells Teiresias to leave.

Analysis:

1. Oedipus is trying to find out who the murderer is.
2. Extracting an answer to a crucial question.

Tools:

To interrogate, plead, reason, level, demand, threaten, accuse.

Scene 2

What the character does:

Oedipus accuses Creon of plotting for the throne.
Oedipus yields to Jocaste to let Creon go.
                    * Beat Change *
Oedipus questions Jocaste about the murder.
Oedipus tells Jocaste about killing the man at the crossroads.
Oedipus suggests that he himself killed Laios.
Oedipus gets Jocaste to send for the shepherd.

Analysis:

1. Oedipus is accusing Creon of wanting to usurp the throne.
2. Exposing a threat to friends.

Tools:

To accuse, warn, lay out the facts, challenge.

Second Beat

1. Oedipus is putting together all of Jocaste's information.

2. Enlisting a loved one's aid.

Tools:

To explain, confess, demand, plead, lay oneself bare.

Here the beat change occurs because Oedipus received new information about Laios that forces him then to reconsider the possibility that he himself may have indeed been Laios' murderer.

Scene 3

What the character does:

Oedipus finds out that Polybos is dead.

Oedipus says he still fears the oracle of his youth.

Oedipus gets information about his past from the messenger from Corinth.

Oedipus demands to talk to the other shepherd.

Oedipus vows to find out about his birth no matter what.

Analysis:

1. Oedipus is resolving the confusion about his past.

2. Looking for the crucial answer to a mystery.

Tools:

To review the facts, hear out a source, form a theory, enlist aid, test someone's credibility.

Scene 4

What the character does:

Oedipus questions the shepherd about his own identity.

Oedipus figures out the truth.

Analysis:

1. Oedipus puts the story of his life together.

2. Making a subordinate confirm a terrible suspicion.

Tools:

To threaten, reason, buck up someone's confidence, put someone at ease.

Exodus

What the character does:

Oedipus tells the chorus about his suffering.

Oedipus asks to be led out of Thebes.

Oedipus says he deserves what he's done to himself.

Oedipus makes up with Creon.

Oedipus asks Creon to take care of his family responsibilities.

Oedipus tells his daughters he is sorry for what they will go through.

Oedipus asks to be sent out of Thebes.

Oedipus asks Creon not to take his daughters away.

Analysis:

1. Oedipus is getting people to help him fulfill his final responsibilities in Thebes.
2. Making sure loved ones will be taken care of.

Tools:

To issue orders, beg, apologize, get a commitment, let friends down easy, teach a lesson.

Through-line

1. Oedipus is saving Thebes from the plague.
2. Taking the best possible care of those entrusted to me.

As this example illustrates, everything you do onstage serves the through-action; anything that does *not* serve the through-action must be eliminated. Keep this thought in mind as you begin to analyze entire plays. (Note: In this example, we derived the through-action from the individual beats. As stated earlier, it is perfectly acceptable to first find the through-action and then fill in the individual beats.)

· · ·

Now that you have been given the necessary tools with which to analyze a text, try them out on a practical problem. Here's a simple scene for you to analyze. Take your time, have fun, and try to come up with several different analyses. We also suggest that you begin immediately to analyze scenes from real plays, because the more you practice, the better you will become at the skills of analysis. We *guarantee* that any scene can be broken down into playable action by this method (see appendix B).

PETE: Your outfit is lovely today.
HARRIET: Do you like it? I thought you would.
PETE: Must have cost you a pretty penny.
HARRIET: Wasn't cheap. You look nice too.
PETE: Thanks. Payday'll do it to you.
HARRIET: Mn-hmm. Always buy a little something to make me feel good.
PETE: The boss held my check back, you know.
HARRIET: Poor thing! Why?
PETE: Er, trouble with serial numbers or something— I don't know.
HARRIET: Why, come on, I'll take you out to dinner.
PETE: No, that's okay, I couldn't—

HARRIET: Well, we could make dinner at my apartment.

PETE: No, I can't, Harriet. Actually, I was hoping you could lend me forty dollars.

If you wish, you can write in your analyses below:

Pete   *Harriet*

1.   1.

2.   2.

3.   3.

1.   1.

2.   2.

3.   3.

3

The Truth of the Moment

As we've already said, the job of the actor is to analyze the text for action and then live truthfully and fully under the imaginary circumstances of the play. To do the latter you must learn to recognize and act upon the *truth of the moment,* or that which is actually happening in the scene as you are playing it. An actor can very easily set in his mind exactly how a scene should be played. This is not the purpose of text analysis, nor is it desirable in terms of execution. *The difficulty of executing an action lies in dealing with that which is actually happening in the other person.* You can't execute your action in general; you must stay in tune with the responses you are receiving. This requires a great deal of bravery and will due to the fact that you can never know exactly what is going to happen next. You must learn to embrace each moment and act on it according to the dictates of your action. As Sanford Meisner says, "That which hinders your task *is* your task."

A good example of what Meisner is talking about is what we call "The Squeaky Door Theory." If your action involves sneaking unnoticed into a room and the door squeaks as you open it, coping with the noise is the true difficulty you face in executing your action. If you ignore it because you feel it inappropriate for the scene, the audience will instantly see that you are ignoring the truth of the moment. In effect, by ignoring the noisy door you stop acting and beg the audience's indulgence until you find a suitable moment to resume.

The same principle holds true in terms of dealing directly with the other person(s) in the scene. Once you've analyzed a scene and decided on a set of tools for the action, *how* you will execute your action—i.e., which tool you will use in a given moment—depends on what is happening in the other person. Just as the squeaky door is the true difficulty you face in sneaking into the room, the other person in the scene is the true difficulty you face in succeeding with your action, because, as we have already noted, the success of a good action is based in the other person. In every moment in the scene you want to find the best way of completing your action based on the other person's behavior. Don't censor or judge your impulses; do whatever occurs to you and don't worry about whether it is appropriate for the scene. There will be times when some of your impulses will end up running counter to your action. For instance, during the course of a scene in which you are *making amends,* you might offend the other person by yelling at him. What you must now deal with is the fact that you've made a mistake. Don't be afraid of trying anything and everything you think would aid your action in a given moment. Allow all your impulses out without censoring or judging them.

Let's say that your action is to *knock sense into a friend.* You have analyzed the scene and decided that you will deliver a certain line "angrily." That preplanned moment in the scene arrives and your partner is doing absolutely nothing to engender anger in you. In fact the feelings that have been awakened in you, over which you have no control, are of a very tender nature. Still you deliver the line angrily. What is the result? First, you have taken yourself out of the scene because you are not dealing with what is happening in the other person or your organic responses to him. Second, your action has ceased to operate, because you are merely portraying the emotional state of "being angry" instead of carrying through with your action based on the exigencies of the *moment.* From the audience's point of view you will appear both wooden and out of sync; after all, nothing *organic* precipitated your angry outburst. To put it simply, you can't fool an audience. They will immediately see that you have acted a lie.

We are not suggesting that you make your choices based on how you think the audience is going to react. Rather, your job as an actor is to be clear; if you manipulate your action in a predetermined way, you will usually be forced to discount the truth of the moment. To live truthfully onstage and effectively perform your action you must learn to embrace each moment *as it actually occurs,* not as you would like it to be. Don't wait until you are comfortable to act; if you develop the habit of depending on emotional oases to get you through, you will develop a limited and predictable repertoire as an actor. Many actors believe that certain emotional peaks are written into a scene and they skim over much of the scene in anticipation of these moments. If you school yourself to act on your perceptions courageously and unhesitatingly, despite the difficulties you face, you will become a forceful presence onstage in every role.

If a given moment makes you angry or sad or causes you to want to reason with the other person, fine. All of these *impulses* are correct; your task is to learn to act on them as they occur in you. In other words, as scary as it sounds, *you must act before you think.* What we mean by this is that you should act on what occurs in you as it occurs in you, without passing judgment on the impulse. The place for applying the skills of analysis is at home. On the stage you can't take the time to question or validate what the scene is engendering in you. If you've taken the time to intellectualize what is happening in any way, the impulse will be lost and your attention will be thrown back onto yourself. Thus you won't be able to perform your action effectively because, again, your focus of attention will not be on what is happening in the other person. If you develop the habit of placing your concentration on the other person, you will be too busy to be self-conscious and all that you do will be in adjustment to the scene and the other actors onstage.

In any demanding activity, your concentration is bound to wander from time to time. This certainly holds true for actors; acting on the truth of the moment for two hours a night is physically and mentally draining work. In those moments when your concentration wanders, gently replace your attention on the other person in the scene. Even the most experienced actor must endure moments of low-level concentration. The worst thing to do in those stressful moments is to in any way chastise or berate yourself. The time you take to say to yourself "Oh, I'm such a terrible actor, I'm so unconnected to what's going on" is simply more time wasted. If you consistently return your attention to where it belongs, eventually it will become stronger and wander less; it will become habituated to the requirements of playing on the stage. Remember, your concentration is like a muscle—training it is no different from an athlete drilling himself to strengthen his muscles. The only way to improve your concentration, your ability to live in the moment, is through assiduous practice. Through practice, it will become second nature for you to place your attention on the other person in the scene. Also keep in mind that replacing your attention on the other person in the scene is the best solution for those moments when you've no idea what to do. That other person will always hold the key as to how to go about executing your action.

Although it is okay to remind yourself of your action if you find yourself lost or confused in a scene, don't constantly compare each moment *to* the action. If you do, it will force your attention back onto yourself and your judgment of how well you are performing. Don't decide as you are playing whether your analysis is correct; commit to it fully and fix it later if something is wrong.

You will never have to become more perceptive to become a better actor. You must simply train yourself to act on your perceptions so that you can fully embrace everything that presents itself to you onstage.

Finally, we would like to point out again that *even nothing is something*. If you are frustrated because your partner is "not giving you anything," *that* is the life of the scene and it is that very frustration you must act on. It is not your job to assess how well the other actor is doing, any more than it is your job to assess how well you are doing. If you are fully committed to your action, what will affect you is the difficulty you face in getting what you want. For instance, if you need to *prevent a friend from making a terrible mistake* and the other actor is barely paying attention to you, don't grumble about what a bad actor he is. Instead, deal directly with the true obstacle you now face—a person who is harder to get through to. If you embrace the difficulty you now face in executing your action, you will find yourself living truthfully in the moment because your inattentive partner will demand your full concentration; all that you do in order to fulfill your action will be in response to his lack of contact with you.

Don't ever feel that you are not being exciting enough; if you are executing your action fully and living moment to moment, you are doing your job. Resist the desire to make things up for the sake of making the scene more interesting; if you do, you will engender in yourself the habit of accepting and creating untruth and hypocrisy.

BEING ALONE ONSTAGE

One of the most difficult acting problems is what to do when you are onstage alone. The question then becomes, Where do you put your attention? How do you gauge the success or failure of your action? There are two possible answers. One is to place the test of the action in the audience—to try and get something from them as if they were in the scene with you. The other possibility is to use your imagination and try to succeed with the person you are using in your as-if from your analysis of the scene. This is like rehearsing in the bathroom mirror before asking someone out on a date. You talk to the mirror as if you were talking to that person you want to ask out. Take, for example, the "To be or not to be" monologue from Hamlet. If you were to use the first solution given above, you might analyze it this way:

1. Hamlet is discussing the pros and cons of suicide.

2. The essential action of that is: getting advice from an objective observer.

3. It is as if I were asking my teacher whether or not he thinks I should get married.

Using this analysis, you would talk directly to the audience so as to get them to tell you what they think you should do.

If you chose the second solution, you might analyze the monologue this way:

1. Hamlet is discussing the pros and cons of suicide.

2. The essential action of that is: untangling an intricate mystery.

3. It is as if my girlfriend suddenly left me, and I'm going over the relationship with my best friend to find out why.

The monologue would then be delivered to some point in the theatre as if you were talking to your best friend in hopes of untangling the mystery. It cannot be stressed enough that this is the only situation where a part of your as-if will enter into what you are doing on stage. Remember not to substitute the as-if for the scene, but rather to use your imagination to play the scene as if you are talking to your friend.

Which solution you use will be based on what will best serve the playwright's intentions, what the director is looking for, and which way will make you perform the action most effectively.

4

Externals

An external is a physical adjustment made by the actor that either aids in the telling of the story or illustrates an imaginary circumstance of the play. A very basic example: you are cast as a king. In all likelihood your crown has nothing to do with your actions; it simply illustrates to the audience that you *are* the king. There are three basic types of externals:

1. Bodily adjustments—for example, posture, voice or speech alterations, and physical handicaps.

2. Ornaments—costumes and makeup.

3. Physical states—for example, drunkenness, exhaustion, feeling hot or cold, or illness.

Invariably, the way to incorporate an external into your work is to make it as habitual as the lines of the play so that it can exist independent of the action.

BODILY ADJUSTMENTS

If you are playing a part requiring you to speak with a German accent, you analyze the script for action and you learn the accent separately. Using a good dialect tape, practice it until it becomes second nature to you. The same goes for vocal quality: if you are playing Othello and the director tells you to be more commanding by working in the lower register of your voice, you must practice until you are able to use that part of your voice automatically.

In the same way, a physical alteration of your body must be worked on until it is habitual. If, for example, you are playing Laura Wingfield in Williams' *The Glass Menagerie,* once you have analyzed the script for action, you then decide on the specific changes you must make in your movement in order to convey that Laura is crippled. Perhaps wearing a heavy leg brace will cause you to walk in a way that evinces her handicap. Or you may have to add certain specific movements. When working with externals, remember that *less is more.* In other words, fulfill the requirements of the script, but don't become bogged down with physical externals to the point that you distract yourself or the audience. Audiences are intelligent and highly suggestible; theatregoers come to the theatre to immerse themselves in illusion. The more attention you call to any theatrical artifice, the less the audience will accept it, because you are calling attention to the artificial nature of the theatre as a whole.

ORNAMENTS

The two types of ornamental externals are costumes and makeup. Neither of these requires a change in either your analysis or your bodily movements. They *may* cause you to move in a certain way, however, because of their inherent restrictions. For example, a person in a suit of armor walks differently from one in tights and a T-shirt.

Ornaments may be specified by the play or suggested by the director, the costume designer, or you. However, you yourself should suggest an ornament only if it helps your action.

An example of an ornament required by the script is in Shakespeare's *Richard III*. Richard is a hunchback. If you're playing him, make sure the hump looks truthful and doesn't impair your performance. To play the part without the hump would be out of line with the intentions of the playwright.

A director may suggest (or demand) an ornament that the script does not call for. For example, you're playing one of the pirates in the *Pirates of Penzance,* by Gilbert and Sullivan, and the director tells you to wear an eyepatch. Will this change your analysis? No. But the audience will infer that you lost your eye in some piratical adventure, and will thus accept you that much more willingly as a pirate. Further, it may add an air of menace to your performance without your having to play menace. This is a perfect example of the illusion that theatre requires to succeed. After all, you haven't actually lost an eye, have you?

Similarly, if you're acting in a period piece, certain

ornaments are necessary to create the illusion of that period in history. Let's say you're playing Thomas More's executioner in *A Man for All Seasons* by Robert Bolt; the designer may ask you to wear a black hood. Does this change your action? No. But it will help preserve the historical accuracy of the play.

Makeup is approached in the same way you approach costume. If you're playing Banquo's ghost during the banquet scene in Shakespeare's *Macbeth,* the script requires that you be drenched with blood. Again, will this change your action? No. But it serves as evidence of Banquo's brutal murder and adds a sense of horror without your having to play horror. Your action plus the given circumstances will create the necessary illusion.

You may need to use makeup unspecified by the script for one of two reasons. First, you may want to illustrate an important facet of the character in order to help tell the story. For example, you're playing Eilert Lovborg in Ibsen's *Hedda Gabler,* and you have to appear as if you've been drinking all night. You might want to use makeup to make your eyes seem red and swollen. Ibsen doesn't stipulate this ornament, but it will have an immediate impact on the audience.

Second, you may want to use makeup for purely technical reasons. For example, the director says you need to wear more rouge on your cheeks because the lights are washing your face out. The other common technical instance occurs when an actor is playing a much older character and needs to convey the illusion of age.

PHYSICAL STATES

The most difficult of the three types of externals are those requiring a physical state. Again, what is necessary is for the audience to perceive the illusion of, say, drunkenness or exhaustion; your job is to create the illusion of these states, not to actually experience them. Let's look at drunkenness, one of the more complicated externals because it demands many physical adjustments and the semblance of a psychological alteration.

To play a drunk scene, you must first figure out what the physical manifestations of being drunk are—for example, slurred speech, wobbly movements, and difficulty maintaining balance. Again, these movements must be made habitual so that you don't have to concentrate on them during the scene. Once you make any physical external habitual it will naturally express itself *through the action*, thus creating an illusion specific to that scene. For instance, if the character is drunk and your action is to *call an aggressor's bluff*, your speech may very well become slowed and overenunciated as you make clear your every word in order to gain the upper hand. If the character is drunk and your action is to *show a friend a good time*, you may very well become expansive and silly.

In the final scene of Herman Wouk's *The Caine Mutiny*, Barney Greenwald drunkenly confronts the officers who brought about Captain Queeg's downfall. This is an excellent example of a scene in which a strong action in conjunction with an external dramatic device creates a rich theatrical illusion.

To approach externals such as being hot or cold or

feeling ill, the principles we have discussed so far once again apply. Here is another hint about how to create the illusions of these states: Look for the means to alleviate them, again allowing the external, if possible, to express itself through the action. A simple example is drawing your jacket closer to you in a scene calling for the illusion of extreme cold.

Let's look again at how a given action affects the form an external might take. If you are in a scene in which you are doing strenuous physical work with some good friends and your action is to *help friends out of a jam,* you might freely wipe off perspiration with your sleeve, unbutton your shirt, loosen your clothing, and so forth. Or if you are playing Blanche DuBois in the trunk scene in *Streetcar* and your action is *holding off a threat,* it might be fitting to dab gently with a handkerchief. Again, the action and the relationship dictate how the external adjustment manifests itself.

After you have found a good action for a scene, it is a good idea to think in terms of the physical activities you might choose to help you execute your action. The difference between physical activities and externals is that a physical activity is a specific bit of stage business the actor chooses to aid his action, whereas an external, as we have discussed, helps to tell the story or illuminate an aspect of the script, and as such is mainly the province of the director and the playwright.

Here are the two guidelines for choosing physical activities:

1. Does the activity specifically aid the action you have chosen for the scene?

2. Does it violate the given circumstances of the play?

(Use your common sense here: You can't use a laser gun if you are playing Athos in *The Three Musketeers*.)

Although there are activities the actor chooses before he actually rehearses or performs a scene, many physical activities are the result of living impulsively in the moment. These spontaneous moments are in essence the fruits of this technique. The best sign that an action is working and that an actor is really living in the moment is when his impulses begin to express themselves through the body uncensored by intellect.

5

Preparing for a Scene

By correctly analyzing your script, you've already done most of the preparatory work for any scene. What remains is to get ready in the moments preceding an actual rehearsal or performance. You don't want to spend any time warming up onstage; you should arrive ready to jump into the scene from the very first moment.

The simplest and most effective way to prepare to do a scene is to go over your analysis. Start with the as-if. Silently talk out what you would say and do in your imaginary situation in order to do your action. Then right before you enter or before the lights come up, state your action to yourself: "I'm going to _____."

A situation that deserves special attention is when a character enters a scene and is confronted by a surprising or arresting set of circumstances. (If you keep in mind that you don't have to actually experience surprise in order to convince the audience that you've come upon something unexpected, then the following technical solutions will be that much easier to employ.)

What you must do is find something to draw your attention from the imaginary circumstances and your knowledge of what you are going to find onstage, since you can't disavow that knowledge. So construct a *preliminary action* for yourself. This is a complete action, arrived at through the analysis process, that creates in you a *false expectation* of what you will actually confront onstage. For example, you are in a scene in which the character you are playing enters and finds his wife lying dead in a pool of blood. Rather than figuring out how to act surprised, analyze the scene:

1. *What is the character literally doing?* Coming home to his wife.

2. *What is the essential action of what the character is doing in this scene?* Planning to make a loved one feel like a million bucks.

3. *What is that action like to me?* It's as if I'm going to see my grandfather to take him out on the town for his seventy-fifth birthday.

To prepare for your entrance, talk over your as-if as you would for any scene and then state your action. The above action is a good one because it is so far from what you will actually encounter onstage. The audience will perceive that you have unknowingly stumbled onto something unexpected *if you clearly make the beat change onstage*; it will read to the audience as the character trying to figure out what to do.

Preliminary actions are also effective if you are waiting onstage for someone and he either enters in an unexpected manner, does not enter at all, or someone else enters instead. The same principles apply: give yourself something more fun and compelling to do than worrying about what is about to happen. Theoretically, you should be able to do this action regardless of whether the other actor ever does make his entrance (something we pray you never have to endure).

LINES

The best advice we can give you about the lines you will be speaking is to learn them *by rote* so that you don't have to concentrate on them while you are playing. We've found drilling the lines while jogging or exercising to be effective because it relieves some of the tedium.

Memorize the lines without inflection and you will avoid the habit of *line readings*—that is, of repeating lines in the same predetermined manner regardless of what is going on in the scene.

THE REHEARSAL PROCESS

Rehearsal should be a place where the actor can experiment with different actions for a scene. You don't have to come up with the perfect analysis for the first rehearsal, but you should come prepared with a workable analysis. Explore different actions for the scene, and explore different tools for the action. Eventually you will have to decide on the best action for the scene, and then your job will become to make that action habitual. Gradually you will be able to concentrate less and less on the verbal, intellectual process of deciding on the best action, and more and more on the intuitive process of working moment to moment off the other actors. Once an action has become habitual, it will simply operate without your concentrating on it. You can then pay attention to what is happening in the moment with the knowledge that your action will guide you.

6

Troubleshooting

This section is a series of questions and answers about problems that may occur while you are working on scenes. This is intended to serve as a guideline. Because scene analysis is a highly personal process, the as-if's have been excluded from the sample analyses when they were not the cause of the acting problem. If an analysis choice is not good for a specific person or scene, the results of the mistake will become obvious in rehearsal. Examples of these cases are among those illustrated in this chapter. You will also find ways to correct your own problems during the rehearsal process.

The problems listed in this section are in reference to act 1, scene 2 from *Two Gentlemen of Verona*.

JULIA: But say, Lucetta, now we are alone,
　　　Wouldst thou then counsel me to fall in love?
LUCETTA: Ay, madam; so you stumble not unheedfully.
JULIA: Of all the fair resort of gentlemen
　　　That every day with parle encounter me,
　　　In thy opinion which is worthiest love?

> LUCETTA: Please you, repeat their names; I'll show my
> mind
> According to my shallow simple skill.
> JULIA: What think'st thou of the fair Sir Eglamour?
> LUCETTA: As of a knight well-spoken, neat and fine;
> But, were I you, he never should be mine.
> JULIA: What think'st thou of the rich Mercatio?
> LUCETTA: Well of his wealth; but of himself, so so.

Q. I'm playing Julia. My action is a strong one, but I'm
totally out of whack with the scene. What went
wrong?
This is my analysis:

1. The character is questioning Lucetta.
2. The action is *making a liar admit the truth.*
3. It's as if . . .

A. You were not specific enough in your first step. Julia
was not simply questioning Lucetta but was asking
for advice on her love life. A poor analysis in the first
step led to your choosing an action incorrect for the
scene, resulting in your problem.

Q. I'm playing Lucetta and am overcome with bore-
dom during the scene. Why does this happen?
This is my analysis:

1. The character is giving Julia advice on her love
life.
2. The action is *giving a gift to a loved one.*
3. It's as if . . .

A. Your action is too passive—a gift can be given with
a single line. It is an errand; once you have given it,

you have nothing else to do for the rest of the scene. That is why you feel so bored. Perhaps you should try *convincing a loved one to accept a gift,* an action you can always actively do.

Q. I'm playing Julia and am overwhelmed with emotion during the scene. Why does this happen?
This is my analysis:

1. The character is asking Lucetta for advice on her love life.
2. The action is *finding the answer to an important question.*
3. It's as if I were asking my mother (who actually had a stroke yesterday) how long she had left to live.

A. The problem lies in your as-if, which is too personal. You are unable to deal with the emotions it arouses in you. Also, it is out of adjustment with the spirit of the scene. This is a lighthearted scene, but your as-if is very serious.

Q. I get caught in the same readings of lines. Why?
This is my analysis:

1. The character is asking Lucetta for advice on her love life.
2. The action is *asking for help.*
3. It's as if . . .

A. The action is too close to your statement of what the character is literally doing. As a result, your action is too general. If your action is in general, then you will act in general. You will slip into line readings in order to try to make the performance work. A possible better action is *getting the lowdown from an expert.*

Sometimes the problem with line readings will occur even if the analysis is correct. Perhaps you *learned* the lines with the inflections in them. Or maybe a great moment happened in one rehearsal and you continue to repeat your lines in the same manner in hopes of re-creating that moment. Truly spontaneous moments can never be re-created. Learn your lines by rote and always have your attention on the other person.

Q. I'm always getting mad at myself during performances when I don't feel I'm acting well enough. Sometimes I even lose track of the scene. What should I do?

A. Don't try to conquer the self-consciousness that inevitably occurs while acting. This is a difficult if not impossible task. Instead, pick an action more interesting to you than worrying about your own performance and use your will to execute it, regardless of how you feel.

Q. My director tells me that I'm faking emotions. Why does this happen?
This is my analysis:

1. The character is asking Lucetta for advice on her love life.
2. The action is *finding the answer to an important question.*

3. It's as if I were asking my friend Flicka which guy she thinks I should go out with.

A. Your as-if is an exact replica of the circumstances of the play. All you have done is substituted Flicka for Lucetta. This forces you into trying to *believe* the events of the play, which makes you "play the scene."

Q. I'm playing Julia and the director tells me that I'm not excited enough during the scene.
This is my analysis:

1. The character is asking Lucetta for advice on her love life.
2. The action is *finding the answer to an important question.*
3. It's as if someone stole my new Rolling Stones record and my friend Evangeline knows who it was, and I just want her to tell me who did it.

A. Although it seems appropriate to the rest of the analysis, your as-if doesn't mean enough to you. This is made evident by your use of the word "just." It's like saying "only"; whatever the word refers to is not all that important to you. You don't really care whether you get the record back.

Q. I'm playing Julia and I'm coming off much too aggressive for the part.
This is my analysis:

1. The character is asking Lucetta for advice on her love life.

2. The action is *finding the answer to an important question.*

3. It's as if someone on the field-hockey team has been beating up my little brother Jordan and I don't know who it is, but I am going to yell at the whole team and stop the jerk who is doing it.

A. Although your as-if means a lot to you, you are not doing the action you listed in your second step. The main element in your as-if is to "stop the jerk who is doing it," not to "find the answer to an important question." You must do exactly what you said you were going to do in step 2.

  If you are having problems that can't be fixed through fixing your scene analysis, your troubles stem from execution. You need to practice your execution skills as listed in the next chapter.

7

The Tools of the Craft

Since we frequently refer to the various tools and skills that you have at your disposal, here is a list of them. Remember that it is within anyone's power to obtain any one of these. All that's involved is hard work and practice.

- A strong clear voice

- Good clear speech

- A strong supple body

- The ability to analyze a scene correctly

- Semantics—the ability to use words specifically in order to choose a good action

- Memorization by rote

- The ability to work off the other person

- The ability to act before you think (i.e., on your impulses)

- The ability to concentrate. Remember that concentration is like a muscle; when it wanders it can only be tempted by a good action and placed lightly back on the task at hand.

- Bravery

- Will

- Common sense

Part Two

PITFALLS (WORKING IN THE REAL WORLD)

8

Introduction

As we stated at the beginning of this book, the actor's job is to live truthfully and fully under the imaginary circumstances of the play. Obviously, this technique is designed to allow you to do exactly that. However, applying the principles we've discussed in a classroom situation is different from employing them in actually working on a play. The principles and tools themselves do not change, but you will be working with people who have little or no idea about the nuts and bolts of this approach to acting. The following chapters are designed to help you work in collaboration with directors and actors with approaches different, perhaps even contradictory to your own.

You don't have to compromise the integrity of your work in result-oriented situations. Sometimes you will be forced to work in a way that seems to violate the commonsense principles discussed in this book. Remember that there are technical solutions to the problems you will encounter. Chapters 9 and 10 point out the major stumbling blocks every actor, regardless of his technique, will face at some point in his career. Chapter 11 offers detailed advice on how to approach these pitfalls both philosophically and in terms of the text analysis formula.

A technique is useless unless it can be called upon in the most difficult and stressful situations.

This method of physical action is a practical one; if it is applied assiduously, it will help you through the most demanding performance and rehearsal circumstances.

9

The Emotional Trap

The single most confusing and upsetting aspect of the actor's work is the so-called emotional life. It is unfortunate that many actors find the emotional aspect of acting so frustrating, because creating emotion is not their concern. There is one simple guideline to follow concerning emotional life onstage: it is beyond your control, so don't worry about it. Ever.

One of the great bonuses of this system of physical action is that every action will give rise to an emotional condition; you won't have to work for it. Once you accept that there is no such thing as a correct emotion for a given scene, you will have divested yourself of the burden of becoming emotional. When you've learned to place your attention on other person, your inchoate feelings about the scene will manifest themselves in a way specific to the moment at hand.

If you work for an emotional result, you will pollute most of what you have learned so far for several reasons. First, if you push yourself into an emotional state you will create an *attitude* that you will then find yourself compelled to maintain throughout the scene. Thus the truth of the moment will be completely lost because your attention will fall on yourself, and your impulses will go out the proverbial window.

Second, you can't execute a physical action while trying to maintain an emotional state. The specificity you've worked so hard for in coming up with a good analysis will no longer operate; you will be acting in general, because your action will be lost in the emotional morass you have created for yourself. Two indications that this is happening are: you lapse into line readings; you find yourself constantly monitoring how well you are doing. Remember, you do not have to feel like performing your action. If you learn to act in spite of what you are feeling, you will bring yourself to life in the scene and develop a strong will in the process.

The third danger is both subtle and ironic. Every once in a blue moon, concentration on the emotions will somehow bring you in line with the needs of the scene. What you must remember is that a technique based on emotion is utterly undependable; because you cannot control what you feel, your emotions can desert you at any time. On the other hand, a technique based on physical action calls upon the *will* and can be used at any time and in any situation, regardless of how you are feeling.

Contrary to popular belief, you need never gear up emotionally for a scene. The idea of emotional preparation is one you need not bother with. As discussed in chapter 5, there are many excellent ways to prepare for a scene that do not require you to whip yourself into a generalized emotional frenzy.

When working onstage, don't take upon yourself the onus of becoming a more "feeling" person. Pushing for emotional results is invariably an attempt to make the scene more "dramatic" or "interesting." Nothing is more interesting or dramatic than an actor working off the truth of the moment, so don't take responsibility for the scene by charging it up emotionally.

Once you've learned to commit fully to a physical action, your only task concerning emotions will be to learn to work *through* them, to let them exist as they will, for they are beyond your control and will come to you quite unbidden. Your emotions are the natural and inescapable by-product of your commitment to your action. Eventually you will learn to work through the torrents of emotion raging through you onstage. Again, your one and only job is to follow through on your *action*.

10

The Myth of Character

As briefly mentioned in chapter 3, it is impossible for you to become the character you are playing. In the theatre, character is an *illusion* created by the words and given circumstances supplied by the playwright and the physical actions of the actor.

Human beings are by nature highly suggestible. If an audience is told that you are the king of France, unless you violate the spirit of the play, it will accept that fact. That you are the king of France is a given; it is your job to find out what being the king of France means to you —i.e., what your actions are.

Aristotle defined character as the sum total of an individual's actions, and his definition holds true for the theatre. Figuring out how you might hold a handkerchief or how many lumps of sugar you should take in your tea does not create a life in you because these things do not necessarily help you fulfill your action. Don't fall into the trap of substituting externals for actions. If you have analyzed a scene correctly for action, you can easily make any external adjustments the director may ask of you. The same holds true for externals demanded by the playwright: *saving a loved one from making a terrible mistake* is a strong action that is as doable with a Polish accent as in your everyday speech.

Be wary of using an external to avoid a difficult problem. If you can't analyze a scene correctly, playing it with a limp and an Australian accent may be superficially entertaining but doesn't solve the problem of what is really happening in that scene.

The reason great actors are so compelling is that they have the courage to bring their personalities to bear on everything they do. Don't ever play a part as someone else would play it. Remember that it is *you* onstage, not some mythical being called the character. For your purposes, the character exists on the printed page for analysis only. If you have done your analysis and memorized your lines, you have fulfilled your obligation to the script and the illusion of your character will emerge. You have the right and the responsibility to bring to the stage who you are. Your humanity is an absolutely vital contribution to any play you act in. Whenever you find yourself worrying about whether you are "doing the character" correctly, reflect for a moment on the words of Stanislavsky: "The person you are is a thousand times more interesting than the best actor you could ever hope to be."

11

Keeping the Theatre Clean

One of the most important tasks an actor faces is working smoothly with the people around him. Each project an actor chooses to work on (and he does *choose*) surrounds him with new personalities, each with opinions about how a scene should work or which acting technique is superior or whether the next day will bring rain. Though conflict is the essence of drama, it is the bane of productivity; therefore, keep the following virtues ever before you: (1) humility, so that when someone corrects you, you will not be offended; (2) generosity, so that when someone errs, you do not condemn, but forgive; (3) consideration, so that when someone believes something, you do not denounce his belief; (4) tact, so that when you believe something, you know the proper place, manner, and time to present that belief. Practice these virtues, and you will rise above petty disturbances and another's opinion will not outrage you. Intuition will tell you which situations to avoid. The best way to prevent conflict is to arrive *prepared*.

Your director is your boss; he has the final say on all artistic matters of the production. Most often he will be delighted to hear your opinion or explain a point to you. If not, it doesn't matter, for you now know what your job entails. Condemning a director for being bad is absurd; you still have to perform. This holds true for the script and the other actors as well. You *should* politely question your director when you need to. But don't pester him and especially don't brashly contradict him in front of the cast. A cast must respect its director, regardless of his abilities. Disrespect results in chaos, and the theatre is a place for order. Conflict with a director should arise only if what he tells you to do impedes the action you must perform, does not pertain to your job as an actor, or is unduly painful or humiliating. If the director suggests you waggle your finger as you recite a speech from *Hamlet,* treat it as you would any external. If the director doesn't understand this technique or condemns it, no matter. You need not mention it to him. Save ideological disputes for the pub. Rehearsal is not a battleground but an incubator.

Treat your fellow actors with the same courtesy you give your director. If an actor has a suggestion, hear him out, for certainly it will have its own logic, and you may benefit by understanding it.

No thought, however heinous, is dangerous. Danger arises only when a reprehensible thought is acted upon. So entertain all thoughts, good and bad.

If a scene demands that you pull an actor's hair, don't really pull it. The object isn't to create pain, but the illusion of pain. There is a proper way to perform stage combat. Truly hurting another actor isn't appropriate for drama and the theatre and will understandably make the injured actor distrust the one who hurt him. Nothing is more contrary to the needs of collaboration. If your character hates another character, don't hate the actor playing that character. The fact that characters disagree is no reason for people to do so. Actors who carry the emotional life of the play offstage and into their own lives are not only wrong but foolish, for they have allowed an imaginary situation to invade their actual life. *Wipe your feet at the door.* What goes on inside the theatre belongs in the theatre. When you leave, leave behind you all the baggage and live your life lovingly. In short, after the show is over, separate yourself from the experiences you have onstage. Conversely, leave worldly cares outside when you come to the theatre to rehearse or perform. Always try to build a rapport with those around you. The closer you are, the freer you'll be to exchange ideas and the better you'll work off the other people in a scene.

Say a director gives you a direction like "be more terrified." Don't inwardly accuse him of being an ignoramus. Instead, go back to your analysis and discover which of the three steps you must alter to give him the effect he desires. Here are some examples:

A. 1. The character is urging Clark to dive off the high board.
    2. The action is *convincing a friend to take a big step*.
    3. It's as if I'm convincing my friend Jim to quit school.

The director dislikes what you are doing and says, "Be firmer." So you change the action and the as-if to:

2. *Making a friend take the plunge.*
3. It's as if I'm making my sister Mary go back to college.

B. 1. The character is asking Mr. Santana for a job.
   2. The action is *convincing a big wheel he could use my help.*
   3. It's as if I walked into Goldstein's Deli and asked, "Do you have any openings?"

Stifling a yawn, the director mutters, "Too dull; be desperate." So you change the action and the as-if to:

2. *Pleading with a hard-nose for a break.*
3. It's as if my dad wants to kick me out of the house and I have no money and nowhere to go.

C. 1. The character is bawling out Margot for her clumsiness.
   2. The action is *putting a jerk in her place.*
   3. It's as if a girl on the subway knocked into me with her umbrella.

The director narrows his eyes and whispers, "I hate it. Be meaner!" So change the action and the as-if to:

2. *Stopping an asshole from turning the tables on me.*
3. It's as if the driver whose negligence had caused my bike accident (and subsequent injuries) was

twisting the story around to make it seem as though *I* had caused the accident.

D. 1. The character is attending his sister's funeral.
   2. The action is *observing the departure of a loved one.*
   3. It's as if my brother, Arthur is moving to Thailand, and I will not see him for years.

Pulling his hair, the director cries, "For God's sake, be sadder!" So you change the action and the as-if to:

   2. *Assuring a loved one of my devotion.*
   3. It's as if my brother Merrill became paralyzed and has been taken to an institution, and he can't respond to my apologies for my bad behavior toward him.

E. 1. The character is refusing Larry's request for a raise.
   2. The action is *letting a subordinate know who's boss.*
   3. It's as if Rob the local plumber is walking in my kitchen and makes a pass at me.

The director slams his clipboard to the floor, throws his hands in the air, and screams, "Why must you be so damned angry at him? Be aloof!" So you change the action and the as-if to:

   2. *Hearing out a subordinate's case.*
   3. It's as if a drunk stumbles up to me and starts telling me why I should give him a dime.

So adjust your steps as needed, in accordance with what the director desires. Now, you will encounter fewer tyrannical directors than compassionate ones, but when you do run into one, you must choose one of three courses of action. The first is to leave the show. The second is to remain and fight him every step of the way by arguing and blatantly disregarding his direction. (This latter is the actor's commonest, cheapest, and most childish weapon.) The third and most productive approach is to say nothing, do as he suggests, and perform your actions as analyzed.

ADVERBS

In some instances, you will be able to satisfy a director's request for a result without changing your analysis. This can be done by performing an action with an adverb chosen to help supply the result the director is looking for. For example, you are playing a scene where the character is telling his wife he's just won the lottery. The action you have chosen is *convincing a loved one I'm on the level,* and it is as if you're telling your brother that your parents are giving you a trip around the world. The director tells you that he needs you to be more excited. Rather than changing an accurate and fun analysis, simply attach to the action the adverb *quickly.* This adverb tells you how you will go about doing the action. It is a *physical, external* adjustment. Another example: Say you are doing a scene where the character is telling his girlfriend that he is leaving her. The action you have chosen is *making a clean break from a friend,* and it is as if you're telling your longtime roommate that you are moving out because things aren't working out anymore. The director asks you to be more sensitive. You might try using the adverb "quietly." This is simply a way of telling yourself how you will physically perform the action.

In choosing adverbs, you always want to look for ones that suggest a physical rather than an attitudinal adjustment. Adverbs such as slowly, loudly, ploddingly, haltingly, are fine. Ones such as jovially, lovingly, maternally, are not, because they require an emotional rather than a physical adjustment. Some adverbs fall between these two clearly defined groups—for example, sloppily, meticulously, exuberantly—and should be used only if the actor feels they do not put him in an emotional state. Remember that adverbs are only a tool to help supply results that a director may ask for; they should not be considered when doing the initial analysis.

. . .

Never direct another actor. If what he does is incorrect in your judgment, discreetly mention it to the director. However, do so only if what he is doing affects *you.* If you are the lead in the play, don't treat the lesser characters as lesser actors or as lesser human beings. The scene you play with the milkman is as important as the scene you play with the queen, and Jonathan is as human as Kathleen.

As far as the stage manager is concerned, he is the lightning rod to your bolts of thunder. His job is a damn hard one. Treat him with respect and deference. If he asks you to do something, do it.

The same is true of the stage crew and all the people working on the show. Being the lead is no excuse for arrogance and incivility. These people, like you, are there to do a good job. Let them.

If you keep the four virtues listed above close to your heart, divergent opinions will not impair your work. When in doubt, remember what the Stoics said: "People are disturbed not by things, but by the views they take of things."

12

Conclusion

We hope this guide has been both useful and fun. After you've digested and begun to apply the principles we've discussed, use this book as a reference. If you are having a problem with some aspect of your work, see if a solution can be found by employing one of the tools or guidelines herein. With time and practice, everything you've absorbed will become an organic part of your work.

There is nothing magical about the craft of acting. Learning to act means becoming physically able to execute the skills we have outlined for you. Acting *is* a set of skills that you can learn with the proper training. Variables such as talent are beyond your control, and, contrary to popular belief, do little to make you a good actor. The natural qualities composing talent that actors are told they must possess—e.g., sensitivity, vulnerability, and high awareness of the senses—are of little consequence for this reason: every human being already has them. What makes an actor a good one is his ability to *act on* the impulses his humanity creates in him.

Many actors have spent their careers trading on, and thus were limited by, their natural talents. Many of these actors had successful careers, it's true, but few grew as artists, because they never took the time to develop a set of skills they could call their own, skills that could never be taken from them. With time, your bag of tricks will either come up empty or become a predictable repetition of itself. How much greater is the self-respect of the man or woman who can call upon the technique he or she has developed over his or her years in the theatre to see him or her through even the most seemingly insurmountable acting problem.

You now have a chance to develop a set of skills that will always be there for you; it doesn't matter if your mother, your father, your boyfriend, or the critic from the *New York Times* is in the audience. As you walk onstage you will be able to say, "I am here to do something worthwhile, and I AM NOT LEAVING UNTIL I DO IT." Then you will be free to really act, and you will see that the actor has the power to move mountains, to inspire courage, compassion, and positive action by his simple willingness to act on what he sees before him. Nothing is more cleansing or exhilarating than watching a human being standing true to his intentions, no matter how impossibly high the odds against him are.

Reading this book alone will not teach you how to act. You must find a way to apply the principles presented herein. (See appendix C.) As simple as they are, we believe it will take you ten or fifteen years to master them, so be patient and gentle with yourself. If you choose to bring the strength of your will and the guidance of your common sense to bear on the task of becoming an actor, then become an actor you will. And if the thought of going into the theatre to perform fills you with excitement and anticipation, you will help to create a theatre that will serve humanity in a loving, powerful way.

Glossary

action: The physical pursuance of a specific goal.

analysis: The process whereby the action of a scene is determined. It is derived from these three questions:

1. What is the character literally doing?
2. What is the essential action of what the character is doing in this scene?
3. What is that action like to me? It's as if . . .

as-if: The answer to question 3 of the analysis. It is a simple fantasy that makes specific for you the action you have chosen in step 2 of the analysis; it is a mnemonic device serving to bring the action to life in you.

beat: A single unit of action. A scene may comprise one or more of these.

beat change: The point during a scene where a new action begins. It occurs when a new piece of information is introduced or an event takes place over which the character has no control and which by its very nature must change what the actor is doing.

cap: The event or condition indicating that an actor has succeeded in doing his action.

character: The illusion created by the words and given circumstances supplied by the playwright and director combined with the actions and externals of the actor.

essential action: The single element that defines what the character is doing in a scene, without which the scene will not work. (*See* action.)

given circumstance: Any piece of information or activity written into the script or demanded by the director comprising the imaginary framework within which an action is performed.

living in the moment: Reacting impulsively to what the other actor in a scene does, according to the dictates of your action.

mnemonic: A device designed to help someone remember something: a fact, idea, condition, etc.

physical activity: A specific bit of stage business the actor chooses to aid his action.

technique: A knowledge of the tools that may be used and an understanding of how to apply those tools.

tools of action: The different ways an actor might go about doing an action.

tools of the craft: The various skills and devices an actor has at his disposal.

through-action: The single overriding action that encompasses all the actions an actor pursues from scene to scene, from the beginning of a play to the end.

Appendix A

The statements made here about respect for the author's words and intention are meant for plays in their final form, where the playwright has provided a script but is not part of the rehearsal process. In situations where a script is being developed through what is commonly referred to as a workshop, many authors welcome actors' comments on everything from word choice to plot structure. When working this way, you must develop a set of ground rules for changing the script at the beginning of the process, so that the integrity of the author is maintained, and once a decision is made it must be held to, because the actor must always remain truthful to the author's intentions.

Appendix B

We have never found a scene that could not be analyzed for action using this method. We have analyzed everything from Shakespeare to the various objects you might find in a child's bedroom. Thus we do not make the guarantee in chapter 3 lightly or with an eye toward self-aggrandizement. It is simply what we have found to be true, based on hundreds of scenes analyzed during countless hours in the classroom. If you come across a particularly difficult scene or you find one you are convinced cannot be analyzed into a playable action, send the scene to us with a self-addressed stamped envelope and we will analyze it for you free of charge. We suggest that you enclose your analysis, or the reasons why you believe the scene cannot be analyzed. Send all inquiries to:

The Authors of *A Practical Handbook for the Actor*
c/o Random House, Inc.
201 East 50th Street
New York, N.Y. 10022

Appendix C

If you've found this book useful, you may want to study these principles in the classroom with professional instruction, as we have had the good fortune to do. As of this writing, the only training program in the country with a program devoted to this particular acting technique is the New York University Undergraduate Drama Department. Based on our personal experience, we recommend this program highly. We believe the best way to thoroughly learn this technique is through intensive study and drill; this book is merely a primer and a reference.

Appendix D

SUGGESTED READING

Aristotle, *The Poetics* (Ferguson translation)
Cicely Berry, *Voice and the Actor*
Bruno Bettelheim, *The Uses of Enchantment*
Epictetus, *Enchiridion*
William James, *Habit*
Marcus Aurelius, *Meditations*
Kostantin Stanislavsky (edited by Elizabeth Hapgood Reynolds), *Stanislavsky's Legacy*

About the Authors

MELISSA BRUDER studied acting at the Stella Adler Conservatory from 1982 to 1984. She then trained with David Mamet and W. H. Macy in their summer acting workshops in Montpelier, Vermont. Her Off-Broadway appearances include Celimène in *The Misanthrope* and Laura in *Look Homeward Angel.* She originated the roles of Amy in *Can't Buy Me Love* and Lisa in *Road Trip,* two original works by Jason Milligan produced by the Action Theatre Group. She is currently a member of the Atlantic Theatre Company, living and working in Chicago, New York, and Vermont.

LEE MICHAEL COHN studied acting at the Drama Studio in London in 1980–81. He received his B.F.A. in drama from New York University, where he studied with David Mamet and W. H. Macy in their summer workshops in Montpelier, Vermont. He has appeared in Off-Broadway and London Fringe productions, including *Romeo and Juliet, Antigone, Long Day's Journey Into Night,* and as "B" in David Mamet's *Yes, But So What.* As co-artistic director of the New York–based Action Theatre Group, he produced and acted in a number of original American plays. Since 1983 he has been a member of the Atlantic Theatre Company. He lives and works in New York City, Chicago and Vermont.

MADELEINE OLNEK is from Connecticut. She made her stage debut at the age of nine as Toto in *The Wizard of Oz.* Her career really began, however, when she started studying with David Mamet and W. H. Macy. She is currently working with the Atlantic Theatre Company in Vermont and Chicago.

NATHANIEL "NED" POLLACK studied at the New York University Drama Department and with various teachers and studios in New York City. He was then lucky enough to hook up with the Practical Aesthetics Workshop. He has also worked with the New Theatre Company, the Goodman Theatre in Chicago, the Atlantic Theatre Company in Vermont, and Playwrights' Horizons in New York City.

ROBERT PREVITO attended SUNY Buffalo and New York University's Undergraduate Drama Department, where he acted in two Mainstage productions, *Hearts in the Highlands* and *Nightmusic.* He is primarily a playwright, however, and has written five plays, all of which have been produced at NYU: *The Restaurant, Priscilla, Omicron, O, Omicron, Jacoda and the Diamond* and *Stake Out.* He is currently a student in the Graduate Dramatic Writing Program at NYU, while at the same time serving as a teaching assistant to the chairman of NYU's Undergraduate Drama Department.

SCOTT ZIGLER is artistic director of the Atlantic Theatre Company, based in Chicago and Montpelier, Vermont. He has been with the company since 1983, and has worked on plays by David Mamet, John Guare, Shel Silverstein and Wallace Shawn, and on original material written by members of the company. He has directed plays by Sam Shepard, Lanford Wilson, Eugene Ionesco, and August Strindberg.